EXPRESS YOURSELF

The One-Year Journal for Girls

Express Yourself

Illustrations by Elizabeth Graeber

WITH TEXT BY KATHERINE FLANNERY

ROCKRIDGE
PRESS

Interior Designer: Liz Cosgrove
Cover Designer: Amy King
Editor: Katharine Moore
Production Editor: Erum Khan
Illustrations © Elizabeth Graeber, 2018

ISBN: Print 978-1-64152-316-5

INTRODUCTION

Journaling is simply the best. In just a few minutes a day, you create a time capsule that you can keep for the rest of your life—which is kind of amazing if you think about it. Next year, next decade, next century (if you're lucky!), you can look back on any day and remember it. You can relive how it felt to be the You that you were at the time. It's sort of like time travel!

But journaling isn't just for future-you: It's great for now-you, too. Reflecting on your day and really thinking it through can have amazing effects. The process of putting your feelings into words and putting those words down on paper can be a huge relief when you've got something bottled up inside. It can maximize your joy when something great happens, and it can reveal surprising things you didn't even know you were thinking.

Since journaling is absolutely private, you can write down anything without worrying about someone judging you. Truths, lies, day-dreams, fears, hopes, likes, hates—you can tell your journal absolutely anything, and it'll just be between you and the paper, unless *you* decide otherwise.

This journal gives you the space to record a year's worth of memories and experiences—just add a few lines each day, and before you know it, you'll have written the story of a year in your life. Along with a blank canvas to jot down your daily thoughts, this journal also gives you an open-ended question to answer each week and a whole set of extra questions at the end of the book to help you sum up your year. Sometimes the questions are just for a laugh, asking you about funny memories or superpowers you wish you had. Others help you get down deep into what makes you tick and what you want most from your future. You can think about these questions all week before you answer them, write a line or two about them each day, or even tackle them the moment you see them. To lend you a little extra inspiration, these pages also include wise words from other super-cool and smart ladies.

As you journal more and more, you'll get to know yourself better and better. You'll get in closer touch with what you like, what you want, how you feel, and who you are. And years from now, when you look back at these pages, you'll see where you once were, which will give you a better understanding of the amazing person you've become.

Really, you're giving yourself the gift of you, which is the best gift there is.

> "Journal writing is a voyage to the interior."
>
> **—Christina Baldwin,** WRITER AND LECTURER

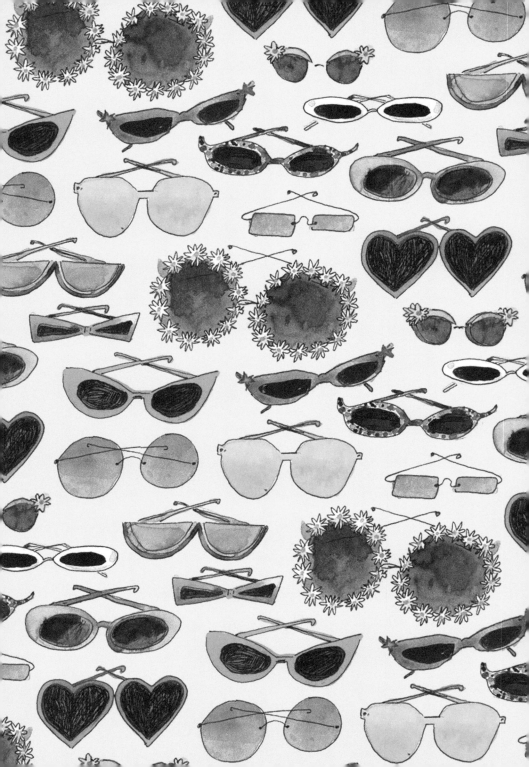

EXPRESS YOURSELF

monday, ___/___/___

tuesday, ___/___/___

wednesday, ___/___/___

thursday, ___/___/___

"THERE'S NO POINT HAVING WISHES IF YOU DON'T AT LEAST TRY TO DO THEM."

—Sally Nicholls, WRITER

friday, ___/___/___

If you could make one wish that was guaranteed to come true, what would it be? How different would your life be once it was granted?

saturday, _____ / _____ / _____

sunday, _____ / _____ / _____

If you could travel anywhere in the world, where would you go? How would you get there? What would be the first thing you did once you got there?

monday, ___ /___ /___

....
....
....
....

TUESDAY, ___ /___ /___

....
....
....
....

wednesday, ___ / ___ / ___

THURSDAY, ___ / ___ / ___

friday, ___ / ___ / ___

SATURDAY, ___ / ___ / ___

sunday, ___ / ___ / ___

"**Traveling is like flirting with life. It's like saying, 'I would stay and love you, but I have to go; this is my station.'**"

—Lisa St. Aubin de Terán, writer

monday, ___/___/___

....
....
....
....

tuesday, ___/___/___

....
....
....
....

What is the funniest, most pee-your-pants-hilarious thing that has ever happened to you?

"YOU GROW UP THE DAY YOU HAVE YOUR FIRST REAL LAUGH— AT YOURSELF."

—Ethel Barrymore, ACTRESS

wednesday, ___ / ___ / ___

thursday, ___ / ___ / ___

friday, ___ / ___ / ___

saturday, ___ / ___ / ___

sunday, ___ / ___ / ___

MONDAY, ___ / ___ / ___

"If you live for having it all, what you have is never enough."

—Vicki Robin, INNOVATOR

tuesday, ___ / ___ / ___

WEDNESDAY, ___ / ___ / ___

thursday, ___ / ___ / ___

FRIDAY, ___ / ___ / ___

saturday, ___ / ___ / ___

SUNDAY, ___ / ___ / ___

Which do you think is more important, doing a job you LOVE, or doing a job that makes you a TON of money? Why?

"Dogs come when they're called; cats take a message and get back to you later."

—MARY BLY, writer

monday, ___ / ___ / ___

tuesday, ___ / ___ / ___

wednesday, ___ / ___ / ___

thursday, ___ / ___ / ___

friday, ___ / ___ / ___

Dogs or cats? Discuss. (If you have allergies, lizards or birds?)

saturday, ___/___/___

sunday, ___/___/___

What is the top thing you think people don't get about you? Are you glad or upset that they don't get it?

monday, ___/___/___

TUESDAY, ___/___/___

wednesday, ___ / ___ / ___

THURSDAY, ___ / ___ / ___

friday, ___ / ___ / ___

SATURDAY, ___ / ___ / ___

sunday, ___ / ___ / ___

"Don't wait around for other people to be happy for you. Any happiness you get you've got to make yourself."

—Alice Walker, activist and writer

monday, ___/___/_____

tuesday, ___/___/_____

Think about the coolest person you know—in real life, a celebrity, anybody. What makes them so awesome? What do you have in common with them?

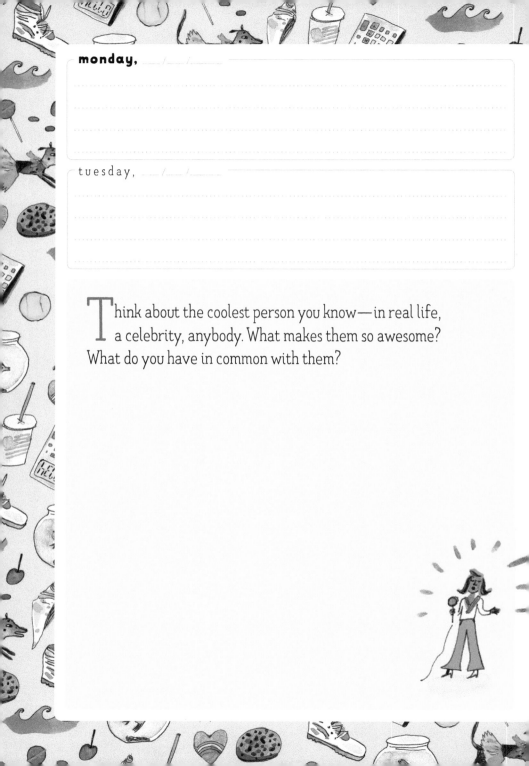

"I CAN'T THINK OF ANY BETTER REPRESENTATION OF BEAUTY THAN SOMEONE WHO IS UNAFRAID TO BE HERSELF."

—Emma Stone, ACTRESS

wednesday, ___ / ___ / ___

thursday, ___ / ___ / ___

friday, ___ / ___ / ___

saturday, ___ / ___ / ___

sunday, ___ / ___ / ___

MONDAY, ___/___/___

"My childhood is a part of my story, and it's why I'm who I am today."

—Misty Copeland, BALLERINA

tuesday, ___/___/___

WEDNESDAY, ___/___/___

thursday, ___/___/___

FRIDAY, ___/___/___

saturday, ___/___/___
....
....
....
....

SUNDAY, ___/___/___
....
....
....
....

What is your absolute best memory from being a little kid?
How do you feel thinking about it?

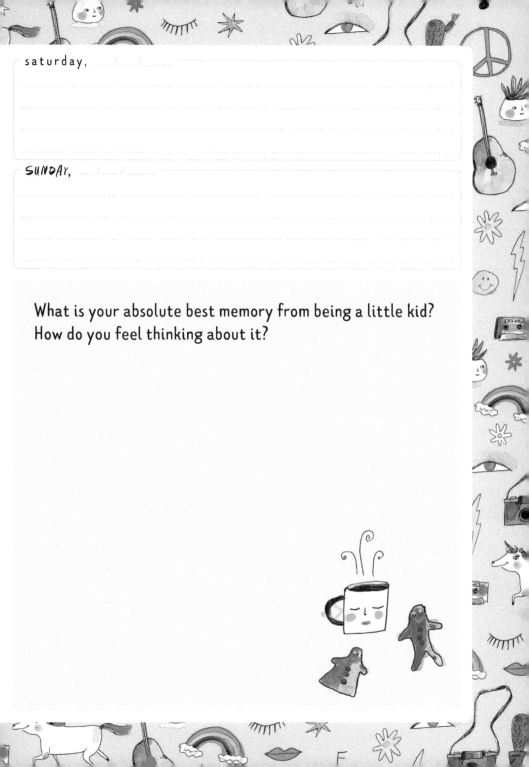

"Anything is good if it's made of chocolate."

–JO BRAND, comedian

monday, ___ / ___ / ___

tuesday, ___ / ___ / ___

wednesday, ___ / ___ / ___

thursday, ___ / ___ / ___

friday, ___ / ___ / ___

If you were a food, what food would you be? Why?

saturday, ___/___/___

sunday, ___/___/___

Do you think love at first sight is possible? Why, or why not?

monday, ___/___/___

....

....

....

....

TUESDAY, ___/___/___

....

....

....

....

wednesday, ___/___/___

THURSDAY, ___/___/___

friday, ___/___/___

SATURDAY, ___/___/___

sunday, ___/___/___

"The advantage of love at first sight is that it delays a second sight."

—Natalie Clifford Barney, writer

monday, ___ / ___ / ___

tuesday, ___ / ___ / ___

What lie have you told that you wish you could come clean about? What do you think would happen if you told the truth?

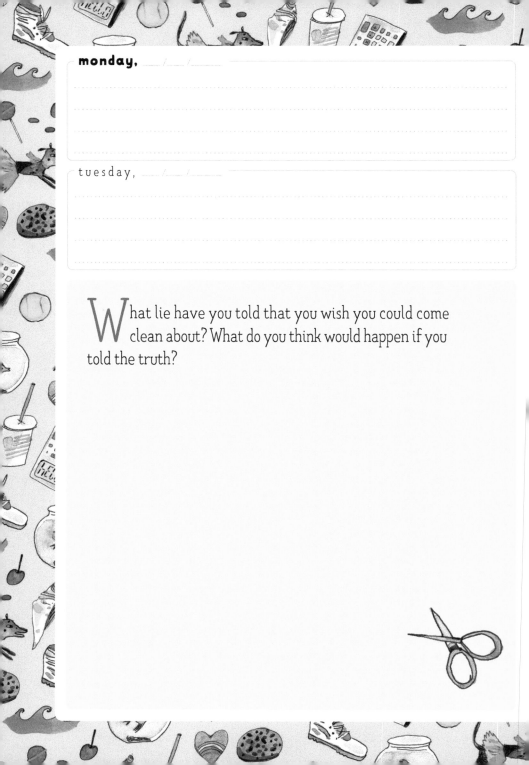

"I TORE MYSELF AWAY FROM THE SAFE COMFORT OF CERTAINTIES THROUGH MY LOVE FOR TRUTH; AND TRUTH REWARDED ME." —Simone de Beauvoir, WRITER AND FEMINIST

wednesday, ___ / ___ / ___

thursday, ___ / ___ / ___

friday, ___ / ___ / ___

saturday, ___ / ___ / ___

sunday, ___ / ___ / ___

MONDAY, ___/___/___

"ACCEPT WHO YOU ARE. UNLESS YOU'RE A SERIAL KILLER."

—Ellen DeGeneres, COMEDIAN

tuesday, ___/___/___

WEDNESDAY, ___/___/___

thursday, ___/___/___

FRIDAY, ___/___/___

saturday, ____ / ____ / _____

SUNDAY, ____ / ____ / _____

What does it mean to you to "be yourself"?

"The most difficult thing is the decision to act. The rest is merely tenacity."

—AMELIA EARHART, pilot

monday, ___/___/___

tuesday, ___/___/___

wednesday, ___/___/___

thursday, ___/___/___

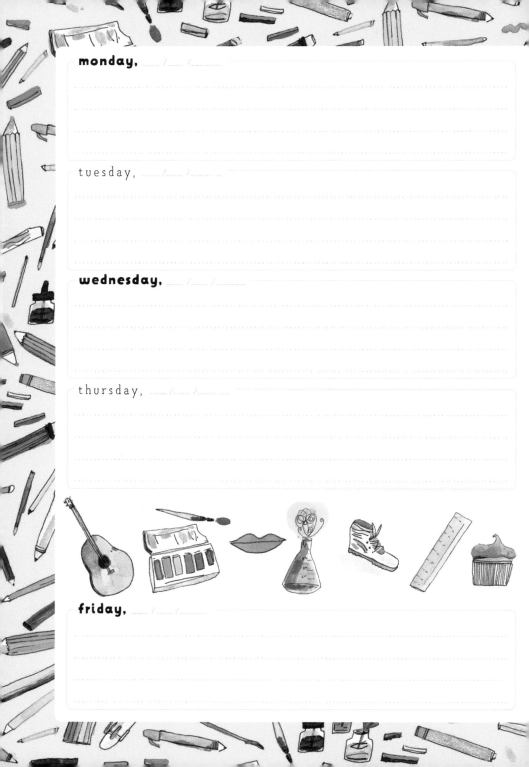

friday, ___/___/___

What is your dream job? How are you going to get it?

saturday, ___ / ___ / _____

....

....

....

....

sunday, ___ / ___ / _____

....

....

....

....

What are the three movies, three books, and three albums you'd take with you if you were going to be stuck on a desert island?

monday, ___/___/___

....
....
....
....

TUESDAY, ___/___/___

....
....
....
....

wednesday, ____ / ____ / ____

....

....

....

....

THURSDAY, ____ / ____ / ____

....

....

....

....

friday, ____ / ____ / ____

....

....

....

....

SATURDAY, ____ / ____ / ____

....

....

....

....

sunday, ____ / ____ / ____

....

....

....

....

"Just the knowledge that a good book is awaiting one at the end of a long day makes that day happier."

—Kathleen Norris, writer

monday, ___/___/___

....
....
....
....

tuesday, ___/___/___

....
....
....
....

What do you like most about school? What would you change about it if you could?

"I'M NOT GOING TO SCHOOL JUST FOR THE ACADEMICS—I WANTED TO SHARE IDEAS, TO BE AROUND PEOPLE WHO ARE PASSIONATE ABOUT LEARNING." **—Emma Watson,** ACTRESS AND ACTIVIST

wednesday, ___/___/___

thursday, ___/___/___

friday, ___/___/___

saturday, ___/___/___

sunday, ___/___/___

MONDAY, ___/___/___

tuesday, ___/___/___

"There's much to be said for challenging fate instead of ducking behind it."

—Diana Trilling, WRITER

WEDNESDAY, ___/___/___

thursday, ___/___/___

FRIDAY, ___/___/___

saturday, ___ / ___ / ___

SUNDAY, ___ / ___ / ___

Do you believe in fate? If not, why not? If you do, what do you think fate might have in store for you?

"People sometimes talk about the power of first impressions, and believe me, there is truth to it."

—ANN BRASHARES, writer

monday, ___ / ___ / ___

tuesday, ___ / ___ / ___

wednesday, ___ / ___ / ___

thursday, ___ / ___ / ___

friday, ___ / ___ / ___

P retend you're someone else and you're meeting you for the first time. What do you see? What's your first impression?

saturday, ___/___/___

....
....
....
....

sunday, ___/___/___

....
....
....
....

Y ou have a choice between two superpowers: flight or invisibility. Which do you choose, and why? What would you do first with your new power?

monday, ___/___/___

TUESDAY, ___/___/___

wednesday, ___ / ___ / ___

THURSDAY, ___ / ___ / ___

friday, ___ / ___ / ___

SATURDAY, ___ / ___ / ___

sunday, ___ / ___ / ___

"The things that make us different, those are our superpowers."

—Lena Waithe, actress

monday, ___ / ___ / ___

tuesday, ___ / ___ / ___

W hat's something you hope will happen in the next year?

> "IF YOU'RE OFFERED A SEAT ON A ROCKET SHIP, DON'T ASK WHAT SEAT. JUST GET ON."
> —Sheryl Sandberg, EXECUTIVE

wednesday, ___ / ___ / _____

thursday, ___ / ___ / _____

friday, ___ / ___ / _____

saturday, ___ / ___ / _____

sunday, ___ / ___ / _____

MONDAY, ___/___/___

"Where Thou art—that—is Home."

—Emily Dickinson, POET

tuesday, ___/___/___

WEDNESDAY, ___/___/___

thursday, ___/___/___

FRIDAY, ___/___/___

saturday, ___/___/___

SUNDAY, ___/___/___

Do you want to live somewhere else when you grow up?
If so, where and why? If not, what do you love about
where you live?

"I had to work very hard, but I did it because I wanted to. That's the real key to happiness."

—ROSALYN SUSSMAN YALOW,
Nobel Prize–winning physicist

$$\frac{2x^2 + 4}{3} = y$$

monday, ___/___/___

tuesday, ___/___/___

wednesday, ___/___/___

thursday, ___/___/___

$$\frac{2x^2 + 4}{3} = y$$

friday, ___/___/___

D

o you want to go to college? What would you study?
If you don't go, what will you do instead of college?

saturday, ___ / ___ / ___

sunday, ___ / ___ / ___

If you could fix one thing about the world, what would it be? How would people's lives be different?

monday, ___/___/___

....

....

....

....

TUESDAY, ___/___/___

....

....

....

....

wednesday, _____/_____/_____

. . . .

THURSDAY, _____/_____/_____

. . . .

friday, _____/_____/_____

. . . .

SATURDAY, _____/_____/_____

. . . .

sunday, _____/_____/_____

. . . .

"There are still so many causes worth sacrificing for. There is still so much history yet to be made."

—Michelle Obama, *lawyer, activist, former First Lady*

monday, ___/___/___

tuesday, ___/___/___

What is your earliest memory?

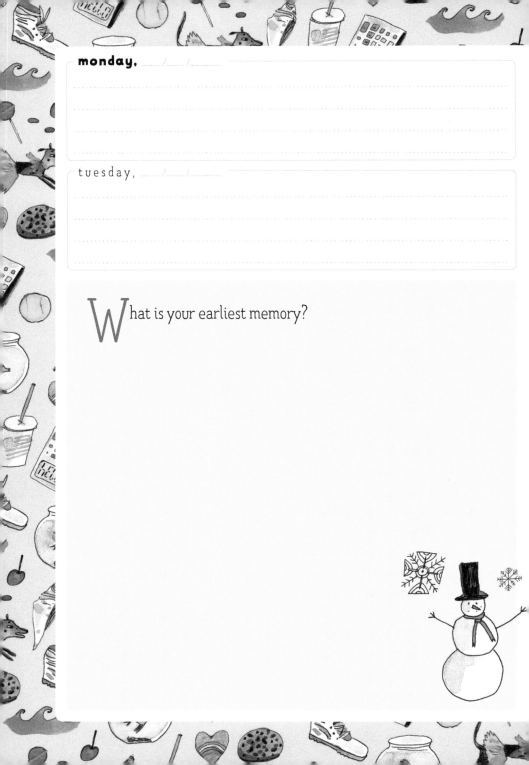

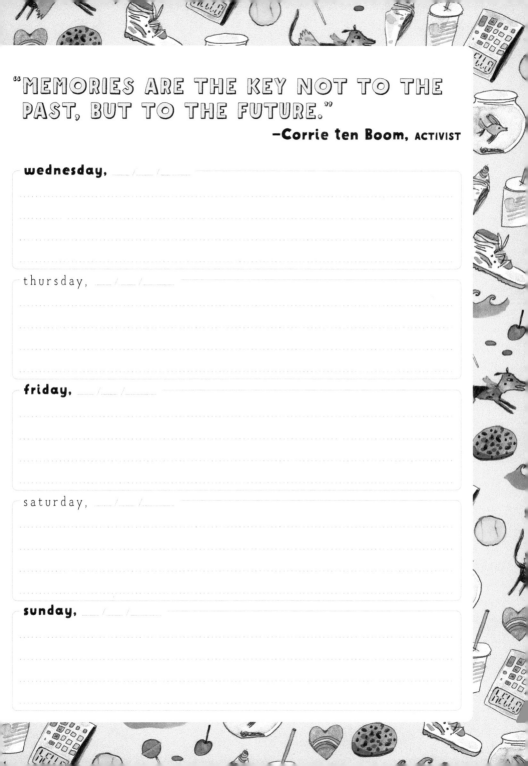

"MEMORIES ARE THE KEY NOT TO THE PAST, BUT TO THE FUTURE."

–Corrie ten Boom, ACTIVIST

wednesday, ___ / ___ / _____

thursday, ___ / ___ / _____

friday, ___ / ___ / _____

saturday, ___ / ___ / _____

sunday, ___ / ___ / _____

MONDAY, ___/___/___

"Parents can only give good advice or put [kids] on the right paths, but the final forming of a person's character lies in their own hands."

—Anne Frank, DIARIST

tuesday, ___/___/___

WEDNESDAY, ___/___/___

thursday, ___/___/___

FRIDAY, ___/___/___

saturday, ___ / ___ / ___

SUNDAY, ___ / ___ / ___

Fill in the blank: My parents are . . .

"**Ah!**
There is nothing
like staying at home,
for real comfort."

—JANE AUSTEN, writer

monday, ___ / ___ / ___

tuesday, ___ / ___ / ___

wednesday, ___ / ___ / ___

thursday, ___ / ___ / ___

friday, ___ / ___ / ___

You wake up in your dream home. What do you see?

....
....
....
....

....
....
....
....

Who is your best friend? What do you love about them?

monday, ___/___/___

....

....

....

....

TUESDAY, ___/___/___

....

....

....

....

wednesday, ___ /___ /___

THURSDAY, ___ /___ /___

friday, ___ /___ /___

SATURDAY, ___ /___ /___

sunday, ___ /___ /___

"It's not that diamonds are a girl's best friend, but it's your best friends who are your diamonds."

—Gina Barreca, writer

monday, ___/___/___

tuesday, ___/___/___

W hat is the weirdest dream you've ever had?

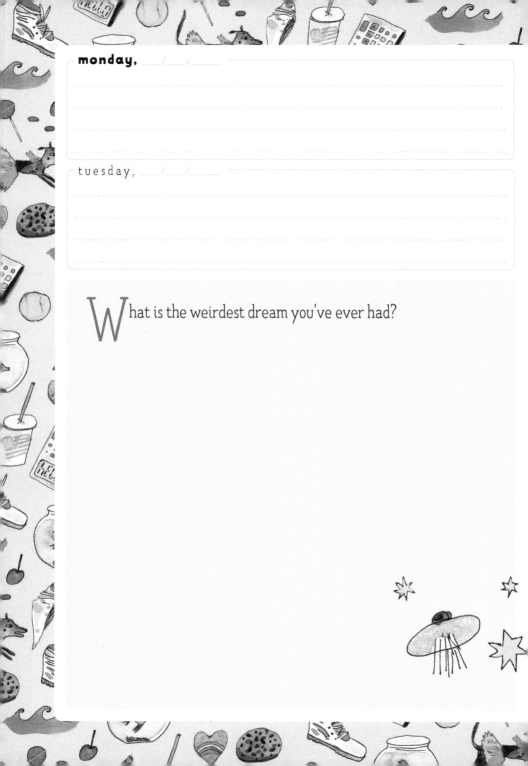

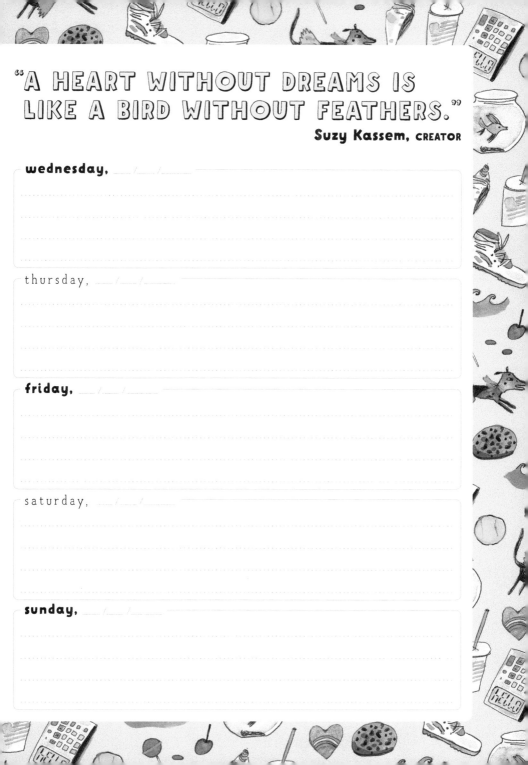

"A HEART WITHOUT DREAMS IS LIKE A BIRD WITHOUT FEATHERS."

Suzy Kassem, CREATOR

wednesday, ___/___/____

thursday, ___/___/____

friday, ___/___/____

saturday, ___/___/____

sunday, ___/___/____

MONDAY, ___/___/___

"You gain strength, courage, and confidence by every experience in which you really stop to look fear in the face."

—Eleanor Roosevelt, LEADER

tuesday, ___/___/___

WEDNESDAY, ___/___/___

thursday, ___/___/___

FRIDAY, ___/___/___

saturday, ___ / ___ / ___

SUNDAY, ___ / ___ / ___

What is your biggest fear? Do you have some ideas on how
to overcome it? What do you think would happen if you
overcame the fear?

"When you love and accept yourself, when you know who really cares about you, and when you learn from your mistakes, then you stop caring about what people who don't know you think."

—BEYONCÉ, musician

monday, ___/___/___

tuesday, ___/___/___

wednesday, ___/___/___

thursday, ___/___/___

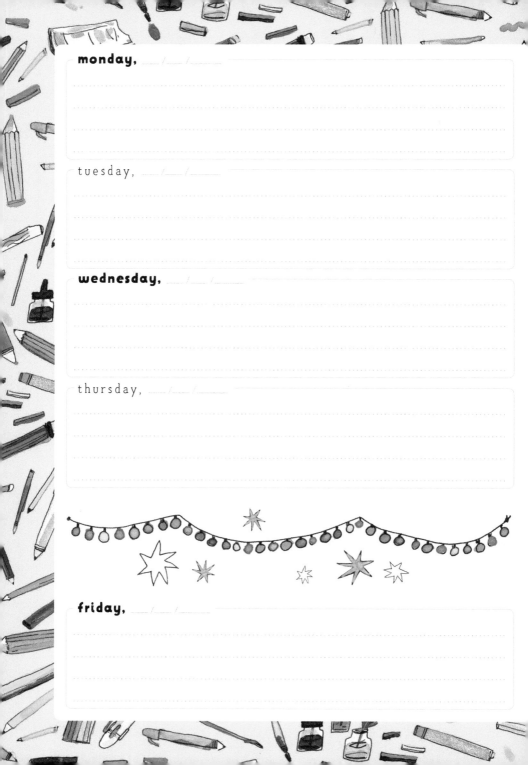

friday, ___/___/___

If you could redo any day of your life, what day would you pick, and what would you do differently?

saturday, ___ / ___ / ___

sunday, ___ / ___ / ___

Do you see yourself as a bit of a comedian, or are you super-serious? Why do you think you're like that?

monday, ___/___/___

TUESDAY, ___/___/___

wednesday, ___ / ___ / ____

THURSDAY, ___ / ___ / ____

friday, ___ / ___ / ____

SATURDAY, ___ / ___ / ____

sunday, ___ / ___ / ____

"When in doubt, make funny faces."

—Amy Poehler, comedian

monday, ____ / ____ / _____

tuesday, ____ / ____ / _____

What would you say to your crush or significant other if you could say anything, no consequences?

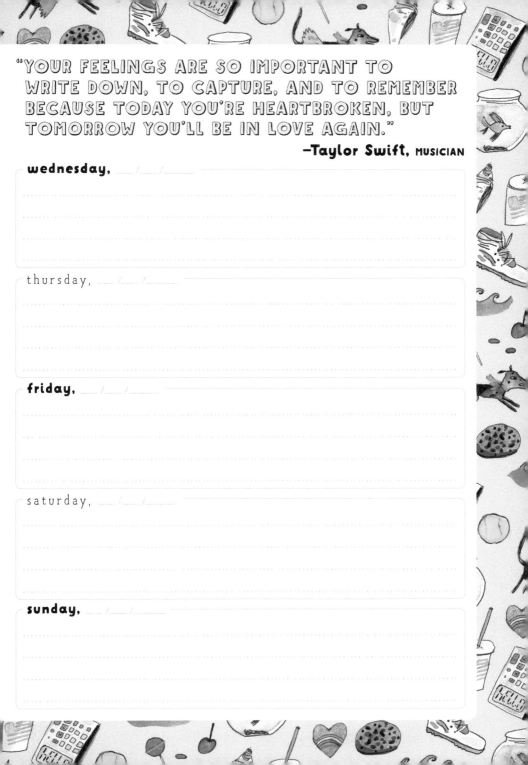

> "YOUR FEELINGS ARE SO IMPORTANT TO WRITE DOWN, TO CAPTURE, AND TO REMEMBER BECAUSE TODAY YOU'RE HEARTBROKEN, BUT TOMORROW YOU'LL BE IN LOVE AGAIN."
>
> **—Taylor Swift,** MUSICIAN

wednesday, ___ / ___ / ___

thursday, ___ / ___ / ___

friday, ___ / ___ / ___

saturday, ___ / ___ / ___

sunday, ___ / ___ / ___

MONDAY, ___ / ___ / ___

"Nobody really cares if you're miserable, so you might as well be happy."

—Cynthia Nelms, WRITER

tuesday, ___ / ___ / ___

WEDNESDAY, ___ / ___ / ___

thursday, ___ / ___ / ___

FRIDAY, ___ / ___ / ___

saturday, _____ / _____ / _____

SUNDAY, _____ / _____ / _____

What is your favorite thing about yourself?

"You can't be that kid standing at the top of the water slide overthinking it. You have to go down the chute."

—TINA FEY, comedian

monday, ___ / ___ / ___

tuesday, ___ / ___ / ___

wednesday, ___ / ___ / ___

thursday, ___ / ___ / ___

friday, ___ / ___ / ___

What's the craziest thing you've ever done?

saturday, ___ / ___ / _____
....
....
....
....

sunday, ___ / ___ / _____
....
....
....
....

Describe your favorite daydream.

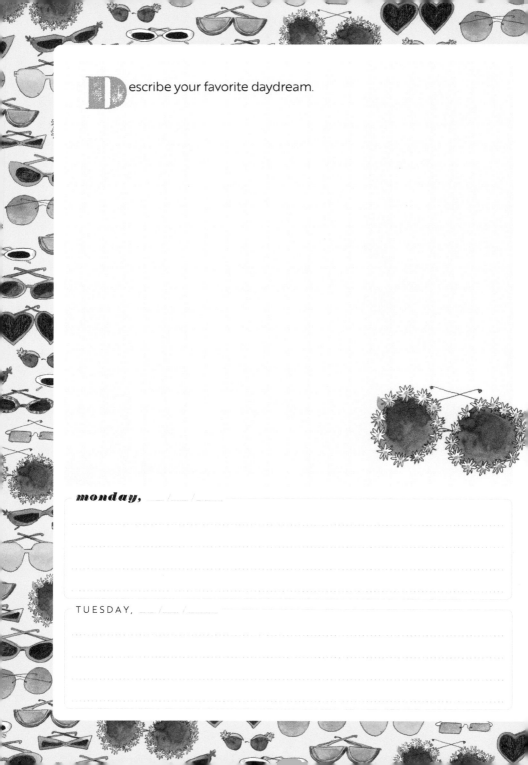

monday, ___/___/___

TUESDAY, ___/___/___

wednesday, ___/___/___

THURSDAY, ___/___/___

friday, ___/___/___

SATURDAY, ___/___/___

sunday, ___/___/___

"It's really splendid to imagine you are a queen. You have all the fun of it without any of the inconveniences and you can stop being a queen whenever you want to, which you couldn't in real life."
—Lucy Maud Montgomery, writer

monday, ___ / ___ / ___

tuesday, ___ / ___ / ___

What's your best habit? What's your worst habit? Do you think you can break it? How?

"POSITIVITY IS LIKE A MUSCLE: KEEP EXERCISING IT AND IT BECOMES A HABIT."

—Natalie Massenet, FASHION ENTREPRENEUR

wednesday, ___ / ___ / ___

thursday, ___ / ___ / ___

friday, ___ / ___ / ___

saturday, ___ / ___ / ___

sunday, ___ / ___ / ___

MONDAY, ___/___/___

"It takes a great deal of bravery to stand up
to our enemies, but just as much to stand up to
our friends."

—J. K. Rowling, WRITER

tuesday, ___/___/___

WEDNESDAY, ___/___/___

thursday, ___/___/___

FRIDAY, ___/___/___

saturday, ___ / ___ / ___

SUNDAY, ___ / ___ / ___

What is something you would do if you were just a little bit braver? How could you get up the courage you need?

"I don't think
any woman
wants to be
known for being
beautiful . . .
I think you want
to be known for
who you are."

—JAMIE LEE CURTIS, actress

monday, ___ / ___ / ___

tuesday, ___ / ___ / ___

wednesday, ___ / ___ / ___

thursday, ___ / ___ / ___

friday, ___ / ___ / ___

I f you could be known for three things, what would you want them to be?

Berry good

saturday, ___ / ___ / ___

sunday, ___ / ___ / ___

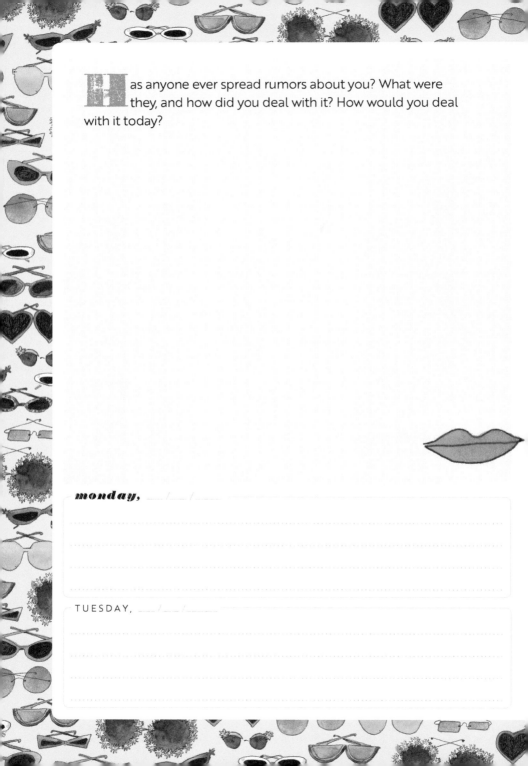

Has anyone ever spread rumors about you? What were they, and how did you deal with it? How would you deal with it today?

monday, ___/___/___

TUESDAY, ___/___/___

wednesday, ___ / ___ / _____

THURSDAY, ___ / ___ / _____

friday, ___ / ___ / _____

SATURDAY, ___ / ___ / _____

sunday, ___ / ___ / _____

"I guess rumors are more exciting than truth."

—Venus Williams, athlete

monday, ___ / ___ / ___

tuesday, ___ / ___ / ___

Would you rather be a bird or a fish? Why?

"FEET, WHAT DO I NEED YOU FOR WHEN I HAVE WINGS TO FLY?"

—Frida Kahlo, ARTIST AND ACTIVIST

wednesday, ___ / ___ / ___

thursday, ___ / ___ / ___

friday, ___ / ___ / ___

saturday, ___ / ___ / ___

sunday, ___ / ___ / ___

MONDAY, ____/____/____

"I have an obsession with Milk Duds. Eating them tastes like heaven."

—Olivia Holt, ACTRESS

tuesday, ____/____/____

WEDNESDAY, ____/____/____

thursday, ____/____/____

FRIDAY, ____/____/____

saturday, ___ / ___ / _____

SUNDAY, ___ / ___ / _____

Fill in the blank: I just can't stop thinking about . . .

you're
invited

"Keep both heart and hand in your own possession, till you see good reason to part with them."

—ANNE BRONTË, writer

monday, ___ / ___ / ___

tuesday, ___ / ___ / ___

wednesday, ___ / ___ / ___

thursday, ___ / ___ / ___

friday, ___ / ___ / ___

D

o you see yourself getting married? If so, what would your married self be like? If not, how do you envision your single life?

saturday, ___ / ___ / ___

sunday, ___ / ___ / ___

What was your first kiss like? Or what do you hope or imagine it will be like?

monday, ___ / ___ / ___

TUESDAY, ___ / ___ / ___

wednesday, ___ / ___ / ___

THURSDAY, ___ / ___ / ___

friday, ___ / ___ / ___

SATURDAY, ___ / ___ / ___

sunday, ___ / ___ / ___

"The first kiss can be as terrifying as the last."

—Daina Chaviano, writer

monday, ___ / ___ / ___

....

....

....

....

tuesday, ___ / ___ / ___

....

....

....

....

Who really gets on your nerves? Why do you think that is?

> "PEOPLE DO NOT WISH TO APPEAR FOOLISH; TO AVOID THE APPEARANCE OF FOOLISHNESS, THEY ARE WILLING TO REMAIN ACTUALLY FOOLS."
> —Alice Walker, ACTIVIST AND WRITER

wednesday, ___ / ___ / ___

thursday, ___ / ___ / ___

friday, ___ / ___ / ___

saturday, ___ / ___ / ___

sunday, ___ / ___ / ___

MONDAY, ___/___/___

"I have always been interested in the paranormal
and afterlife, everything from ghosts to angels.
I think that everyone has that curiosity of the
great unknown."
　　　　　　　　　　—Hilary Duff, ACTRESS AND WRITER

tuesday, ___/___/___

WEDNESDAY, ___/___/___

thursday, ___/___/___

FRIDAY, ___/___/___

saturday, ____ / ____ / ____

SUNDAY, ____ / ____ / ____

Do you believe in an afterlife? If so, what do you think it's like? If not, what do you think happens when people die?

"Having children makes you see the world in a completely different way."

—LINDA RONSTADT, musician

monday, ___/___/___

tuesday, ___/___/___

wednesday, ___/___/___

thursday, ___/___/___

friday, ___/___/___

Do you want to have kids? Why or why not?

saturday, ____ / ____ / ____
....
....
....
....

sunday, ____ / ____ / ____
....
....
....
....

What is something you can't believe you actually got away with?

monday, ___/___/___

TUESDAY, ___/___/___

wednesday, _____/_____/_____

....
....
....
....

THURSDAY, _____/_____/_____

....
....
....
....

friday, _____/_____/_____

....
....
....
....

SATURDAY, _____/_____/_____

....
....
....
....

sunday, _____/_____/_____

....
....
....
....

**"All I really want to do are things
I haven't done ... See what I can
get away with."**

—Sia, musician

monday, ___/___/___

tuesday, ___/___/___

Fill in the blank: I'd lose it if my crush walked up to me and said . . .

"THE MARK OF A TRUE CRUSH, WHETHER THE OBJECT BE MAN, WOMAN, OR CITY, IS THAT YOU FALL IN LOVE FIRST AND GROPE FOR REASONS AFTERWARD." —Shana Alexander, JOURNALIST

wednesday, ___/___/___

thursday, ___/___/___

friday, ___/___/___

saturday, ___/___/___

sunday, ___/___/___

MONDAY, ___/___/___

"I looked in the mirror and said, 'You're either going to love yourself or hate yourself.' And I decided to love myself. That changed a lot of things."
—Queen Latifah, MUSICIAN AND ACTRESS

tuesday, ___/___/___

WEDNESDAY, ___/___/___

thursday, ___/___/___

FRIDAY, ___/___/___

saturday, ___ / ___ / ___

SUNDAY, ___ / ___ / ___

How do you feel about your body?

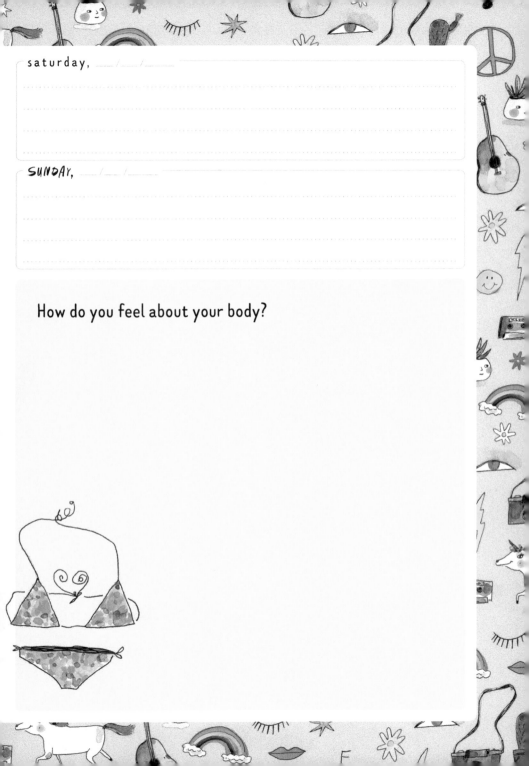

"Any mature,
responsible adult
doesn't run around
stomping their feet
and screaming,
'I'm a mature,
responsible adult.'"

—DEBBY RYAN, actress

monday, ___ / ___ / ___

tuesday, ___ / ___ / ___

wednesday, ___ / ___ / ___

thursday, ___ / ___ / ___

friday, ___ / ___ / ___

What cool qualities do you have now that you hope to still have as an adult?

saturday, _____ / _____ / _____

sunday, _____ / _____ / _____

What is the scariest thing that's ever happened to you?

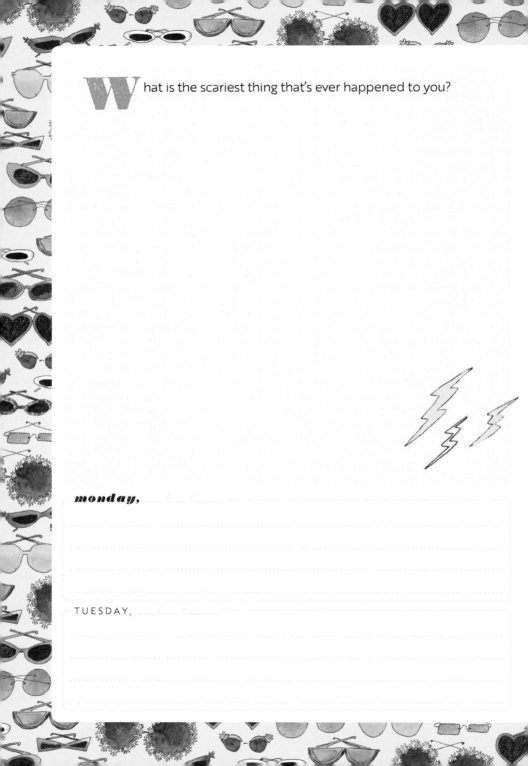

monday, ___/___/___

....
....
....
....

TUESDAY, ___/___/___

....
....
....
....

wednesday, ___/___/___

THURSDAY, ___/___/___

friday, ___/___/___

SATURDAY, ___/___/___

sunday, ___/___/___

"I'm not afraid of storms, for I'm learning how to sail my ship."

—Louisa May Alcott, writer

monday, ___/___/___

tuesday, ___/___/___

W hat would you like to get better at? What can you do to get there?

> "NO MATTER WHO YOU ARE, NO MATTER WHAT YOU DID, NO MATTER WHERE YOU'VE COME FROM, YOU CAN ALWAYS CHANGE, BECOME A BETTER VERSION OF YOURSELF." **—Madonna, PERFORMER**

wednesday, ___ / ___ / ___

thursday, ___ / ___ / ___

friday, ___ / ___ / ___

saturday, ___ / ___ / ___

sunday, ___ / ___ / ___

MONDAY, ___/___/___

"Let us make our future now, and let us make our dreams tomorrow's reality."
—Malala Yousafzai, ACTIVIST AND NOBEL LAUREATE

tuesday, ___/___/___

WEDNESDAY, ___/___/___

thursday, ___/___/___

FRIDAY, ___/___/___

saturday, ___ / ___ / ___

SUNDAY, ___ / ___ / ___

What are you most looking forward to in the next year?

END-OF-YEAR Q&A

Can you believe it's been a year since you started this journal? Think back over the past year, and take some time to answer the following questions about your life over the last 12 months. You might even want to go back and read some of your journal entries. That's one of the best things about journaling, after all—you've captured it, and now you can go back and reflect on it.

1. What can you do now that you weren't able to do a year ago?

2. What is the biggest thing that's changed in your life over the past year?

....

....

....

....

....

....

....

3. What is your best memory from the past year?

....

....

....

....

....

....

....

....

....

....

4. Did you go on any trips this year? If so, where to?

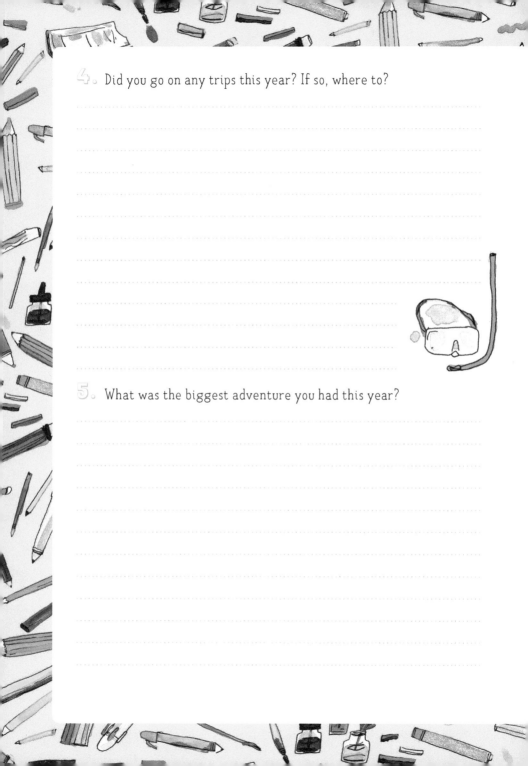

5. What was the biggest adventure you had this year?

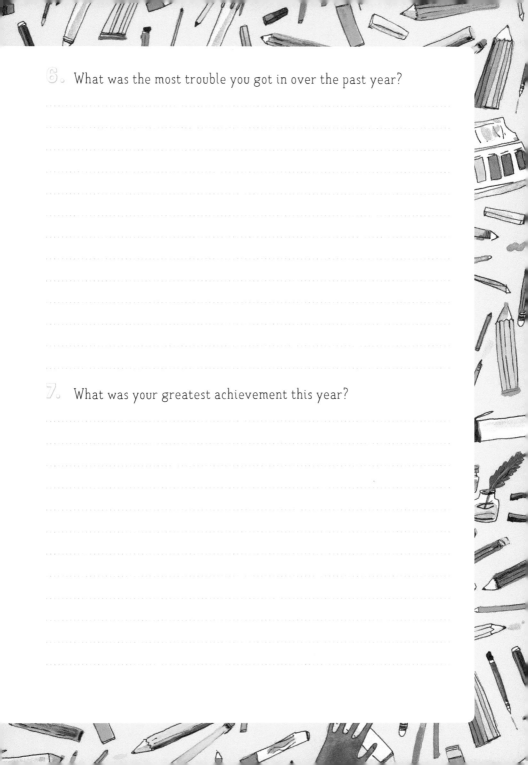

6. What was the most trouble you got in over the past year?

7. What was your greatest achievement this year?

8. What was the funniest thing that happened to you this year?

9. If you could change one thing about this past year, what would it be?

Pink

10. What's something that you couldn't live without now but that you didn't have a year ago?

....
....
....
....
....
....
....
....
....

11. What was the hardest thing you went through this year?

....
....
....
....
....
....
....
....
....
....
....

12. Did you make any new friends this year? Did you lose any friends this year?

13. If you could relive one day from this past year, which one would it be?

14. What has been your most important relationship this year?

15. What was the worst fight you got in this year?

16. What surprised you most this year?

17. What did you outgrow this year?

18. What are some new responsibilities you took on this year?

19. What did you love most about this past year?

20. Which of your journal answers from the past year surprises you most? Why?

ABOUT THE ILLUSTRATOR

Elizabeth Graeber is an artist and illustrator living in the DC area with her husband and two small dogs. She always liked drawing in sketchbooks and still does today. See samples of her work on her site www.ElizabethGraeber.com.

ABOUT THE AUTHOR

Katherine Flannery is a writer and editor living in New Jersey with her husband, dog, and fighting fish. She had a mohawk as a teenager and remembers it being both the hardest and absolute best time of her life. Her journals from those years are now precious to her. She just wishes she had more of them.

CPSIA information can be obtained
at www.ICGtesting.com
Printed in the USA
BVHW050949091218
535158BV00017B/397/P

9 781641 523165